What's the Issue?

WHAT'S FREEDOM OF THE PRESS?

By Katie Kawa

KidHaven
PUBLISHING

Published in 2020 by
KidHaven Publishing, an Imprint of Greenhaven Publishing, LLC
353 3rd Avenue
Suite 255
New York, NY 10010

Designer: Andrea Davison-Bartolotta
Editor: Katie Kawa

Photo credits: Cover (top) noraismail/Shutterstock.com; cover (bottom) Robert Kneschke/ Shutterstock.com; p. 5 (top left) Dmitri Ma/Shutterstock.com; p. 5 (top right) LightField Studios/ Shutterstock.com; p. 5 (bottom left) Cozine/Shutterstock.com; p. 5 (bottom middle) Syda Productions/Shutterstock.com; p. 5 (bottom right) ymgerman/Shutterstock.com; p. 6 courtesy of the National Archives; p. 7 Michael Nigro/Pacific Press/LightRocket via Getty Images; p. 9 Mandel Ngan/AFP/Getty Images; p. 11 (inset) MPI/Getty Images; p. 11 (main) Frank L Junior/ Shutterstock.com; p. 13 (top) Ink Drop/Shutterstock.com; p. 13 (bottom) Mark Reinstein/Corbis via Getty Images; p. 15 Rehman Asad/Barcroft Images/Barcroft Media via Getty Images; p. 17 Jim Watson/AFP/Getty Images; p. 18 © iStockphoto.com/swapnacreative; p. 19 FrameStockFootages/ Shutterstock.com; p. 21 David M. Schrader/Shutterstock.com.

Cataloging-in-Publication Data

Names: Kawa, Katie.
Title: What's freedom of the press? / Katie Kawa.
Description: New York : KidHaven Publishing, 2020. | Series: What's the issue? | Includes glossary and index.
Identifiers: ISBN 9781534530034 (pbk.) | ISBN 9781534567382 (library bound) | ISBN 9781534531277 (6 pack) | ISBN 9781534567399 (ebook)
Subjects: LCSH:United States. Constitution.–1st Amendment–Juvenile literature. | Freedom of the press–United States–Juvenile literature.
Classification: LCC KF4774.K39 2020 | DDC 323.445–dc23

Printed in the United States of America

CPSIA compliance information: Batch #BS19KL: For further information contact Greenhaven Publishing LLC, New York, New York at 1-844-317-7404.

Please visit our website, www.greenhavenpublishing.com. For a free color catalog of all our high-quality books, call toll free 1-844-317-7404 or fax 1-844-317-7405.

CONTENTS

The News You Need to Know   4

Freedom and the First Amendment   6

The Fourth Branch   8

Freedom or Safety?   10

Limits and Laws   12

Not Always Free   14

Problems in the United States   16

True or Fake?   18

Worth Fighting For   20

Glossary   22

For More Information   23

Index   24

The News You Need to Know

When people want to know what's going on in the world, they often turn on a TV news show, pick up a newspaper, or visit a news website. In the United States, these news **sources** and the people who work for them—also known as the press—have the right to freely share **information** with their audience. This is called freedom of the press, and it means the government can't stop them from telling the truth.

Why is a free press so important, and why do some people think it's in danger? Read on to find out!

Facing the Facts 🔍

In 1787, future U.S. president Thomas Jefferson wrote, "Were it left to me to decide whether we should have a government without newspapers, or newspapers without a government, I should not hesitate a moment to prefer the latter." This means he believed it was more important to have a free press without a government than to have a government without a free press!

radio news reports

TV news shows

What's the press?

magazines

newspapers

news websites

Freedom of the press **protects** these and other news sources. The people who report the news—often called journalists—sometimes have to fight for the freedom to inform, or educate, people about what's happening in their country and around the world.

5

Freedom and the First Amendment

The idea of freedom of the press didn't start in the United States. The first law that officially protected the press was passed in Sweden in 1766.

Less than 30 years later, the United States included this freedom in the Bill of Rights. This part of the U.S. **Constitution** is a list of the first 10 amendments, or changes, to the document, which were written to make sure certain rights couldn't be taken away. Freedom of the press is part of the First Amendment. Other First Amendment freedoms include freedom of speech and freedom of **religion**.

Facing the Facts

The Bill of Rights was ratified, or formally approved, on December 15, 1791.

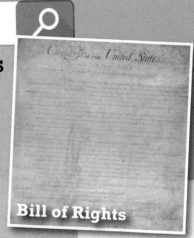

Bill of Rights

The Bill of Rights was written more than 200 years ago, but the freedoms it protects, including freedom of the press, are still important issues in the United States today.

The Fourth Branch

The U.S. government has three official branches. The legislative branch makes the laws, the executive branch makes sure the laws are carried out, and the judicial branch **interprets** the laws. A system of checks and balances is meant to keep each branch from getting too powerful.

Some people call the press the fourth branch of the government. This is because the press is another part of the system of checks and balances. Journalists tell citizens the truth about their leaders. This holds those leaders **accountable** for their actions and decisions.

Facing the Facts

People sometimes use what they learn from the press to petition the government—to ask leaders to fix things they feel are wrong. The right to petition the government is another freedom granted by the First Amendment.

8

Journalists want to help citizens know as much as possible about the people in charge of their country, so they ask leaders hard questions about things they've done. Sometimes leaders might not like what the press reports about them, but it's important for them to remember that the press has a job to do too.

Freedom or Safety?

Many Americans, including many leaders throughout history, have believed the United States can only stay safe and strong with a free press. Other leaders, though, believe giving the press too much freedom can make the United States less safe.

For example, in 1971, President Richard Nixon tried to stop major newspapers from printing parts of secret documents about the **Vietnam War** called the Pentagon Papers. Nixon believed this was a national security problem, but the U.S. Supreme Court ruled that the newspapers had the right to freely share this information.

Facing the Facts

When a person or government tries to control what the press prints or tries to stop the press from printing something, it's called censorship.

The 1971 Supreme Court ruling in the case of *New York Times Company v. United States* allowed the *New York Times* and other newspapers to continue reporting on the Pentagon Papers. The Supreme Court felt it was more important to protect the freedom of the press than to keep information secret for security reasons.

THE SECRET HISTORY OF THE VIETNAM WAR

THE COMPLETE AND UNABRIDGED SERIES
AS PUBLISHED BY
The New York Times

THE PENTAGON PAPERS

BASED ON INVESTIGATIVE REPORTING BY NEIL SHEEHAN.
WRITTEN BY NEIL SHEEHAN, HEDRICK SMITH, E. W. KENWORTHY AND FOX BUTTERFIELD
WITH KEY DOCUMENTS AND 64 PAGES OF PHOTOGRAPHS

Limits and Laws

Does freedom of the press mean journalists can write whatever they want? Although the press has a lot of freedom, there are certain things the government can stop them from sharing. Libel is the printing of false information about a person to cause them harm, and it's not protected by the First Amendment. When libel is spoken, such as on a radio or TV show, it's called slander. This is also not protected.

Student journalists face their own limits on free speech. In 1988, the Supreme Court ruled that school officials have the right to remove articles from school newspapers.

Facing the Facts 🔍

The 1964 Supreme Court case *New York Times Company v. Sullivan* changed libel laws in the United States. Before this, a person only had to prove a statement was false for it to be considered libel. However, the Supreme Court ruled in this case that if a statement is about a public figure, they need to prove that it's false and that the person who printed it knew it was false.

One of the biggest problems facing the press today is the fight against fake news. Many news stories that aren't true are still protected by the First Amendment, so they continue to be **published**, especially online. It's often up to individuals to learn which sources to trust.

Not Always Free

Not every country values a free press the same way the United States does. Although the United Nations (UN)—a group that fights for rights around the world—lists freedom of the press as a basic human right, some countries don't protect this right. The governments of these countries, such as China and North Korea, strongly censor their press.

Journalists in countries that don't have a free press are often in danger. In 2018, more than 250 journalists were put in jail around the world. That same year, at least 34 journalists were murdered for doing their job.

Facing the Facts

In 2018, more journalists were put in jail in Turkey than in any other country. The country with the highest number of journalist deaths that year was Afghanistan.

As more countries have started to limit freedom of the press, more journalists have been put in jail or killed. Many people are speaking out about this problem and are working to make the world safer for journalists.

Problems in the United States

Journalists face many **challenges** in countries that don't have a free press. However, they also face challenges in the United States. President Donald Trump has often spoken out against what he believes is unfair reporting about him, and he's called for stronger libel laws.

President Trump has sometimes used strong language to talk about journalists he feels aren't doing their jobs correctly. He's called them the "enemy of the people." However, many people believe this kind of language goes against the idea of a free press.

Facing the Facts

In 2018, five people were killed in a shooting at the *Capital Gazette* newspaper office in Annapolis, Maryland. The journalists who **survived** the shooting worked to put out a newspaper the next day to prove that nothing can stop a free press from sharing information.

President Donald Trump has said he could take away reporters' **access** to White House press events if they don't follow certain rules or act in a way he feels is right. Some people believe he has the right to do this, but others believe this goes against the First Amendment.

True or Fake?

President Trump has called certain news sources "fake news." Fake news is a real problem, but many people—from world leaders to average citizens—also use those words to describe true stories they don't like. People who fight for freedom of the press believe this use of "fake news" causes citizens to be less likely to trust any news sources. This makes it easier for governments to censor the press.

Even if people don't like what the press is reporting, it's important to respect their right to report it. That's what living in a free country is all about!

Facing the Facts

May 3 is World Press Freedom Day. This is a day the UN has set aside to honor the work done by journalists and to call attention to places in the world that still don't have freedom of the press.

Rights come with **responsibilities**. Journalists have the right to freely share information, but they also have a responsibility to make sure their reporting is fair and truthful. Most journalists work hard to be trustworthy and would never write a fake news story.

Worth Fighting For

Freedom of the press has been part of life in many countries for a long time, but some people are worried it won't be around forever. Censorship, attacks on journalists, and the number of journalists put in prison have all been on the rise. However, there are many individuals and groups around the world who are working to protect journalists and their freedom to report the truth.

A free press keeps citizens informed, holds leaders accountable, and allows many different voices to be heard. It's a freedom worth fighting for!

Facing the Facts

In August 2018, more than 300 newspapers in the United States published opinion pieces from their editors about the importance of a free press. This movement was led by the *Boston Globe* newspaper in Boston, Massachusetts.

WHAT CAN YOU DO?

Learn more about freedom of the press in the United States and other countries.

Sign up to work on your school's newspaper.

Learn how to tell the difference between a fake news story and the truth.

Watch or read news stories with a trusted adult, and talk about what you learned.

Respect the freedom of the press, even if you don't like what a news story is reporting.

Raise money for groups that protect freedom of the press around the world.

If you're interested in this issue, these are some of the many ways you can get more involved. It's never too early to start standing up for important freedoms!

GLOSSARY

access: The ability to use or have something.

accountable: Required to explain actions or choices.

challenge: A problem.

constitution: The basic laws by which a country, state, or group is governed.

information: Knowledge or facts about something.

interpret: To explain the meaning of something.

protect: To keep safe.

publish: To print a written work and present it to the public.

religion: A set of beliefs about a god or gods.

responsibility: A duty that a person should do.

source: A person, place, or thing from which something comes or where it can be found.

survive: To keep living.

Vietnam War: A war fought between North Vietnam and its allies and South Vietnam and its allies, including the United States, from the 1950s to the 1970s.

FOR MORE INFORMATION

WEBSITES

America's Founding Documents: The Bill of Rights

www.archives.gov/founding-docs/bill-of-rights

This part of the National Archives website features facts about the First Amendment and the rest of the Bill of Rights, as well as pictures and the full text of the document.

News Literacy Project

newslit.org

News literacy skills help people decide which news sources to trust, and the News Literacy Project's website features quizzes and tips to sharpen these skills.

BOOKS

Down, Susan Brophy. *Free Press and Censorship*. New York, NY: Crabtree Publishing Company, 2018.

Hoover, Stephanie. *Freedom of the Press*. New York, NY: Gareth Stevens Publishing, 2017.

Machajewski, Sarah. *American Freedoms: A Look at the First Amendment*. New York, NY: PowerKids Press, 2018.

INDEX

B
Bill of Rights, 6, 7
Boston Globe, 20
branches of
    government, 8

C
Capital Gazette, 16
censorship, 10, 20

F
fake news, 13, 18,
    19, 21
First Amendment, 6,
    8, 12, 13, 17

J
Jefferson, Thomas, 4
journalists, 5, 8, 9,
    12, 14, 15, 16,
    18, 19, 20

L
libel, 12, 16

N
*New York Times
    Company v.
    Sullivan* (1964),
    12
*New York Times
    Company v. United
    States* (1971), 11
Nixon, Richard, 10

P
Pentagon Papers, 10,
    11

S
security, 10, 11
slander, 12

T
Trump, Donald, 16,
    17, 18

U
United Nations (UN),
    14, 18
U.S. Constitution, 6
U.S. Supreme Court,
    10, 11, 12